Dedicated with love to Moran & Eric Chajmovic
and their delightful kids: Yoni, Roni & Eden- Li.

Your friendship, kindness, wisdom and warmth
make the world a better place.

The Bill of Rights is the name for the first ten amendments to the United States Constitution, which limit the power of the federal government and guarantee citizens of the United States certain rights. These amendments were ratified on December 15, 1791, when 3/4 of the states agreed that they were fair, during the presidency of our first president George Washington. James Madison (1751-1836) was one of the founding fathers of the United States and wrote the Bill of Rights. Later on he served as the fourth US president from 1809 to 1817.

2nd Amendment

Right to bear arms (own guns)

3rd Amendment
Government can't lodge troops in private homes.

4th Amendment

The government cannot come into your home unless it has legal permission from a judge.

6th Amendment
The government cannot hold you in jail for a long time without a trial if you are accused of having broken the law.

CONNECTICUT AVENUE

JAIL

VISITING

7th Amendment
Jury trial in civil cases involving money.

GRAND JURY

IN SESSION

8th Amendment

The government cannot punish you for a crime in a cruel and unusual way.

The United States of America

10th Amendment

The government cannot claim to have more power and authority than what the Constitution permits, and all other powers not listed in the Constitution belong to the states or individuals.